IT'S NOT A
Perfect World,
BUT I'LL TAKE IT

IT'S NOT A
Perfect World,
BUT I'LL TAKE IT

50 LIFE LESSONS FOR TEENS LIKE ME
WHO ARE KIND OF (YOU KNOW) AUTISTIC

JENNIFER ROSE

Skyhorse Publishing

Skyhorse Publishing books may be purchased in bulk at special discounts for sales promotion, corporate gifts, fund-raising, or educational purposes. Special editions can also be created to specifications. For details, contact the Special Sales Department, Skyhorse Publishing, 307 West 36th Street, 11th Floor, New York, NY 10018 or info@skyhorsepublishing.com.

Skyhorse® and Skyhorse Publishing® are registered trademarks of Skyhorse Publishing, Inc.®, a Delaware corporation.

Visit our website at www.skyhorsepublishing.com.

10 9 8 7 6 5 4 3 2 1

Library of Congress Cataloging-in-Publication Data is available on file.

Cover design by Rain Saukas
Cover photo: iStock

Print ISBN: 978-1-5107-0549-4
Ebook ISBN: 978-1-5107-0550-0

Printed in the United States of America

Contents

PREFACE
My life (so far)

I WAS BORN ON AUGUST 1, 1996 in New York City. In 2000, I was diagnosed with autism. As a child, I was very high functioning. In fact, my father even tried, though unsuccessfully, to get me into the gifted program at my elementary school. I was also very creative and enjoyed making up stories in my head based on my favorite cartoon characters. I even created my own personal newspaper that I called *The Backpack News*.

But I still had a learning disability and didn't talk very much. When I did talk, it was mostly to obsess about the various cartoons I liked. In 2005, I started biomedical treatments, which included chelation therapy, a gluten-free diet (which I hated), dietary supplements, and a hyperbaric oxygen chamber (which I kind of liked).

However, things took a turn for the worse in the sixth grade. While moving from elementary to middle school is a difficult transition for everyone, it's especially challenging for someone with special needs. I was having difficulty with certain subjects, and there was friction with some teachers. With the help of a counselor, my mom recruited several girls from school to be my friends and help me adjust to the new environment. These girls were called "Jenny's Angels," and they made a big difference. I even had a huge party with them once. Another bright spot for me during this year was meeting Jenny McCarthy at an AutismOne conference.

I was mostly fine in the seventh grade, though somewhat introverted. I worked at a snack bar with my mom, and I joined the Newspaper Club. I even made a few friends. I was showing some interest in shopping and pop music—like a typical girl my age. When spring came along, however, I developed allergies, and these led to many emotional outbursts. When it rained on the last day of school and field day was canceled, I completely lost it. Luckily, I was still able to have fun the following week during my family's trip to Toronto.

Eighth grade was awful. In addition to school stress, I was also preoccupied with preparing for my bat mitzvah. In the end, I had to leave my middle school, because I was so overwhelmed. At my next school, the environment was not very friendly. For example, at one point, I was trying to sharpen a pencil, but the teacher wouldn't let me. Eventually, she even unplugged the sharpener, and I lost it. I was so agitated that I couldn't think straight—I even (believe it or not) called the police on my parents one night after an argument.

Nothing could prepare my parents for what would happen next, however. After one huge outburst, they finally saw the light and decided to take me to an alternative school for special needs kids. (Three different schools in a few months!) I was still having some emotional issues and worried about getting kicked out, but started talking about these issues with a therapist and seemed to be on a more even keel. I managed to stay at that school for a whopping three and a half years. I made close friends, got a boyfriend, and worked with and donated to various charities. I went on fun trips to amusement parks and museums with my friends and one day even got to see the set of *Jersey Shore*. I tried my hand at Tae Kwon Do, fan fiction, acting, and even swimming. Now I finally had the time and energy to focus on my goals.

Despite these improvements, I still had one big problem—dealing with mean girls. Some would pick on me and call me stupid, even if they acted nice toward everyone else. Sometimes I got so upset that I cried myself to sleep at night. However, both the principal and my mother said that the reason the mean girls hated me so much was that they saw me as a threat to their popularity, and that the best thing to do was to ignore them. Good lesson, no?

By the eleventh grade, it became clear that this school was way too easy for me. In fact, nothing exciting happened that year, except Hurricane Sandy. Since the power was knocked out at home, Dad took the family to eat at the cafeteria at Drew University, where he teaches. I noticed how cute the boys were there.

In the twelfth grade, my parents sent me to a school that was more academically rigorous. I was having issues with reading too slowly, which was very taxing, especially since I was working on my SATs and failed twice. Luckily, my parents found an eye doctor who was able to fix the problem.

In the summer of 2014, I got my first real job: an internship in the library at a residential summer camp for special needs kids, Camp Ramapo. I had previously gone there as a camper for about five years with my younger sister, and I made a few good friends there.

I was eventually accepted into college, but it proved to be quite a challenge. I decided to be daring and take five courses my first semester, but ended up having to drop one course due to the work-load. I also struggled during my second semester, getting agitated and doing poorly on tests.

But I am otherwise doing great. I am turning my love of writing into a writing major. I am also writing for fun, as well as working on the computer, watching both classic and contemporary movies, and doing charity work.

PART I
DREAMS AND REALITY

LESSON 1
Life is not a straight line

MY VERY FIRST DAY OF SCHOOL was in September 2001. I graduated from high school in June 2014, and by then I wasn't the same person I was when I was five. While this may seem obvious, it's actually a pretty vital life lesson. As Tyra Banks says, "The road to success is not a straight line, it's a zigzag line." Okay, she was talking about modeling, but it still applies to the more low-key world of real life. How? Well, I went through a lot during my thirteen years of schooling. From being the only special needs student in my public school class to attending a school for high-functioning autistic and Asperger's kids and now going to college, it was one long journey.

The road was pretty bumpy along the way. I had to deal with loneliness, bullying, and behavioral problems. But I had plenty of positive things to help me along, from ideas for writing movies to my friends who supported me. Along the way, I picked up many life lessons. And you know what? I'm still learning. In fact, I didn't understand some things until very recently, like how to handle my boyfriend's really dumb (and endlessly repeated) jokes. I will learn more stuff as I get older—when I'm thirty and a mom, for example. Moms are always learning new things. They have to. Just ask any mom.

These life lessons are the lessons that truly stick, not the facts like when the Civil War happened or who was president at the end of World War II. I learned those things in school, but they don't really have any effect on my life. It doesn't really matter whether or not I remember the trivial facts. (Don't tell that to my dad; he's a history professor.)

Lessons about doing what I can set my mind to, on the other hand, or about not listening to negative comments, or even about embracing my differences—that's what truly matters. They're even more important considering that, since I have autism, the road has been bumpier for me than for most teens. Especially since I've been trying to be as normal as possible for most of my childhood! Of course, the bumps are what makes life life.

I wrote this book to share my stories and to help teens of all abilities. I explain my life experience and the lessons I learned along the way. If you are a teenager, you're probably dealing with issues involving your dreams, your school, your family, your friends, life in general, and maybe autism. Here's how I dealt with them.

LESSON 2
Not all your dreams
will come true . . .

EVER SINCE I WAS LITTLE, I wanted to act. I was drawn to the glamour and the fame, of course, but another big reason for it was that I felt so disconnected from the outside world: for me, reality was like watching a movie. So I wanted a TV series about me. My favorite child actresses were Abigail Breslin, Dakota Fanning, and Kristen Stewart. I was particularly impressed by how much these girls achieved before they were old enough to vote. In fact, Abigail Breslin was the exact same age as I!

At first, I was too shy to tell my parents about my ambitions, but when I was eleven I told them I was worried I would get too old before a company discovered me! My parents reassured me that it was a common fantasy for kids and that it would pass, but I refused to listen. I wanted to be like the glamorous people on TV. So. Freakin'. Bad.

In the eleventh grade, there was one girl I knew who did sports, music, and acting. She even claimed to be an extra for the Disney Channel. I was so very bored at school that I really wanted to start acting. One day, I found a website online that promised to make me famous. "Cool! This must be the same website that made that girl famous," I thought. I used a form on the website to send in my information, in case they wanted me.

Several months later, the company called. They asked to speak to my parents, at which point Mom and Dad told me it was probably a scam website. (The company wanted me to pay to work for them.) I knew that I shouldn't be fooled by these websites, but I didn't want to give up on my dream. So I eventually found another website, one without a price tag. But even then my dad told me, "Now, Jenny, if you wanted to be a doctor, you wouldn't start by operating on your little sister. You would have to be trained first." He suggested that if I *really* wanted to act, I could check out the theater department in college.

Offering another reality check, Dad also told me, "These child stars have agents to help them find work." I did have my mom, who put me in a movie, *Bought*, but that was a documentary, and documentaries can feature ordinary people. In fact, most of them do.

Moral of the story? If your dreams seem too good to come true, they probably are. Also, most acting websites are just scams. And if you want to act at a young age . . .

Rule #1: Live in an "acting place" like Hollywood or New York. You know, not Morristown, New Jersey.

Rule #2: Come from an acting family, or at least a family that works in the entertainment industry. (My dad says he had an acting career "that lasted about 45 minutes." I can believe it.)

Rule #3: Really, don't live in New Jersey.

Rule #4: Being autistic means you have to work harder. Autistic people lack focus and are often very shy. I can relate to computers—in fact, I'm kind of a geek—but actors in movies and plays need to relate to other actors.

Rule #5: So, if you're autistic and you want to act, focus, focus, focus on people, people, people.

Rule #6: For goodness' sake, do NOT live in New Jersey.

There's nothing stopping me from having an acting career in the future, but it will take work, not just dreams. It won't automatically come to me in a neat glamorous package.

LESSON 3
. . . at least not overnight

SPEAKING OF CHILDHOOD DREAMS, I also loved the semi-popular video game series *Backyard Sports*. I liked its characters, in particular, because they were very complex for a kiddie sports game: one was a rock-and-roll fan, another was a sassy tomboy. I wanted to create a movie based on this game, and I imagined cartoons and stories about the Backyard Kids (multicultural kids between the ages of five and ten who played sports together, while saving the world and doing normal kid-stuff as well). But over time—eight years, in fact—my movie and story ideas evolved into a composition involving rock music, superheroes, and boy-girl crushes. I even wrote a story and posted it on DeviantArt, a website where anyone can put up their creative work.

Now, how was I going to make a movie? New Jersey isn't exactly a film industry Mecca. Not that that stopped me at first. I called Lani Minella, who did most of the voices for *Backyard Sports*. I told her about my idea, and she seemed to appreciate it, especially since Hollywood has been getting pretty creatively bankrupt. (I called her the same year two movies about Snow White were released. Two Snow Whites in one year? Seriously?)

Unfortunately, she thought that it was a rather obscure franchise and that it would be easier to make a film based on a more popular franchise, like Batman. She told me it might become a TV show, but not a movie. (I assumed a TV show about *Backyard Sports* would last only one season.)

Anyway, Lani gave me an idea for a college project. Eventually, I found a blog by a young boy who wanted to create a *Tales of the Backyard Kids* web series and asked people to donate ideas. I suggested that we do parody shorts about my favorite movies, including *Pitch Perfect*, *The Breakfast Club*, *The Mask of Zorro*, *Titanic*, and even *Dr. Jekyll and Mr. Hyde* (the Spencer Tracy version). He said these were fantastic ideas, and I am in the process of writing the scripts.

All this goes to show that you should have a big dream, even if it doesn't come true quickly or in the form you'd originally envisioned. If you work toward a big dream for a long time, it will change so much that eventually it will no longer be the same dream you had when you began. But that's how all great ideas evolve.

LESSON 4
Some dreams work for you, and some don't

WHEN I WAS A LITTLE GIRL, I wanted to be a writer, but I never fully realized it. I would make up stories in my head and write stories, but I never thought about a career as a writer. At least not for a while.

When I was thirteen, I was mature enough to start thinking about my dreams more consciously. Inspired by my favorite female singers, like Avril Lavigne, Natasha Bedingfield, Hilary Duff, and Kelly Clarkson, I wanted to become a musician myself. I was obsessed with popular music and found it a safe haven during difficult times.

So I looked around and found a website called Taltopia.com, where regular people could show off their talents in acting, music, and comedy. Someone was looking for musicians for a soundtrack to a film he was making, so I called him up. "You're a musician?" he said. "Oh cool, you can just send us some of your music, and we'll take it from there."

I was excited to become a musician, but I couldn't compose any songs because I didn't have any actual instruments. Also, I didn't really know how to compose a song. And I couldn't write music. Otherwise, I had everything it takes.

So I decided to buy some songs online. I wanted to make a CD of me singing along to my favorite songs, such as Britney Spears's ". . . Baby One More Time," Hilary Duff's "Fly," Avril Lavigne's "When You're Gone," and Pink's "Who Knew."

However, I eventually realized that despite practicing the songs over and over again, I was too shy to record an album at home, especially with Mom and Dad around to hear me. I was afraid they might dance to the music, and that would be super embarrassing. And my singing skills weren't all that great.

I still wanted to be a musician, though. In the ninth grade, my friend Kurt (name changed to protect the edgy) and I wanted to make a band called "Smashing Cellos," a pun on the band Smashing Pumpkins. My musical tastes were already maturing—my favorite musicians were the Beatles and Elton John, so we tried to model ourselves after them.

We didn't get far. While I continued to fantasize about being a musician, eventually I realized that writing is more my forte, so I focused on writing fan fiction. Being a writer was the dream that lasted and matched what I was actually good at, though it took time to figure this out. Some aspirations are fleeting, but others are permanent, and you should focus on the second kind.

LESSON 5
Use your dreams to make a difference

ANOTHER LASTING DREAM has been the dream of making a difference. When I was sixteen years old, I entered an essay contest sponsored by Lowe's Home Improvement store. The contest's prompt asked, "How do you make improvement in the world?"

Now, that wasn't too hard for me to answer. I'm improving the world in a lot of ways. I work with a company called DoSomething.org, which encourages teenagers to do projects such as charity work and energy conservation. I have collected "Jeans for Homeless Teens." ("How about Homes for Jeansless Teens?" my dad asks. More on dad jokes later.) I've done some environmental activism, a video about musical education, and two school supply drives. I also support websites like Change.org (where people can sign petitions for the causes they believe in), Water.org (which helps bring fresh water to Third World countries), Feeding America (which helps poor families put food on the table), and Credo Action (an activist phone company).

I also volunteer at a special needs camp to help out with the younger kids. My little sister is autistic, more seriously affected than I am, so I have to be supportive of her. When my family is out shopping and my sister gets hyperactive, I calm her down. My mom says I have a gift for understanding autistic children. That's because I've been there.

However, I also do good for the world in another way. I write stories to entertain people. These are fairly rough times, and in difficult times art is often what helps people get through. Take the Great Depression of the 1930s, for instance. Back then people had many wonderful movies that were pure escapism: *Horse Feathers* and *The Wizard of Oz*, just to name a few. However, original movie ideas these days are running low. We have some great movies, such as *The Amazing Spider-Man* and *Frankenweenie*, but most are awful (I'm thinking of *The Oogieloves in the Big Balloon Adventure* here).

This is a shame, since it doesn't take much to make a great movie. All it needs is a fun plot, good acting (star-studded cast optional), a lot of heart, and, if it's a musical, great songs. Instead, we are getting either gross-out "comedy" or gross-out horror, or a movie geared toward five-year-olds without much to entertain parents and older kids.

I think I have plenty of original ideas up my sleeve, such as *Hollywood High*, a film about an actor who becomes a schoolteacher and uses his acting talents to help his pupils develop their personalities. I have also tried to write a story based on my favorite TV series, *Manimal*. It was about a handsome rich doctor who can turn into an animal to help police solve crimes. (The series lasted like eight episodes before it was canceled, and you can see why if you look up the trailer. It's camp, which means it's so bad, it's funny.) I hear a *Manimal* movie is on the way, and I would love to work on the script. Especially with my favorite actor, David Tennant.

I also use my writing to help kids. There was a boy on my school bus who had Asperger's, and he had the dream of writing a fantasy story about boys who fight evil pop stars. I helped make that dream come true for him by writing the story on DeviantArt. True, I did most of the work, but he gave me the idea, and in Hollywood you get credit for that.

So you see, you can do good in many ways: with activism, stories, movie ideas, and understanding children. Charity can take on any form you like, and you can use your dreams and talents to make a difference.

PART II
SCHOOL

LESSON 6
Some teachers don't just help you learn; they make an impact

FOR MOST KIDS, TEACHERS are old people who ramble on and on about facts, kind of like the teacher in *Ferris Bueller's Day Off.* They tell you exactly the kinds of trivial things I mentioned in the first lesson. However, there are also cool teachers, even for the kids who hate school. They are the ones who teach you the things that matter.

In the seventh grade, I didn't have a lot of friends, but I had an awesome teacher, Mr. O'Brien. (Name changed to protect the fabulous.) He was really funny and made history really entertaining by making jokes. In fact, he reminded me of Jon Stewart from *The Daily Show.* One day he joked, "Warren Harding's close friends were in his cabinet. For example, the guy down the block was his treasurer!" Another time he said, "After Prohibition was repealed, all the Irish were happy again" (he could say this because he's Irish). If more teachers made subjects like history entertaining, kids wouldn't be so obsessed with pop culture trivia.

He also joked about wanting to be president, which I took to heart. This was when Barack Obama became president, and he had an "if-I-can-make-it-anyone-can" image, what with being the first African American in the White House. Because I was a very literal person and because I enjoyed having something exciting in my life, I took my teacher's words very seriously. From drawing pictures of Mr. O'Brien as president to asking Mom and Dad if a schoolteacher could become president, I took what he said and ran with it. This fantasy really kept me entertained for a while.

He was without a doubt one of my favorite teachers from the middle school years. And he really went out of his way to help, inviting me to study sessions on the mornings before tests. When you don't have a lot of friends your age, having a caring teacher really helps.

One day at the end of the seventh grade, when I was upset because field day was canceled, he gave me an awesome book called *32 Third Graders and One Class Bunny*. It was about the ups and downs of being a teacher. When I read it, I couldn't stop laughing! It's amazing what a laugh-out-loud book can do. And in the eighth grade, when I got to have him as a teacher again, he was lending out his little teddy bear to his students, the way some schools lend out their school rabbit. (Notice the reference here?) His bear even got to have a sleepover with my own teddy bear!

Some teachers are just there to help you learn, but others leave more of a mark on your life. They do it in their own little ways, from reaching out to help students who are different to making subjects entertaining. The most important lessons he taught me were that you should reach out and help people and that laughter is a great way to do that.

LESSON 7
Hard work pays off

WHILE THE ELEVENTH GRADE wasn't exactly the most challenging year for me (because I'd switched to a less demanding school), my teachers still kept me busy with projects. I did a report on toads, a project about shopping for a house, a report about *Hamlet* in pop culture, and last, but certainly not least, a project on genetic diseases.

I worked very hard on that last one over the course of several days. (I still took a break to go grocery shopping with Dad, which is always fun because I like hanging out with him.) I was nervous about the project because I wasn't used to doing big assignments on weekends. There was also additional stress that weekend because I was also attending an open audition for the Disney Channel, even though I thought I had no chance of being called back. (Right again!)

I did a lot of research for the project, both in books and online. (Yes, some people still use books!) I had to learn how to do PowerPoint and how to work with an outline. I had to study polycystic kidney disease, Marfan syndrome, cystic fibrosis, Duchenne muscular dystrophy, and Turner's syndrome.

It was a really busy weekend. However, when I finally turned the project in, my teacher said he enjoyed it and gave me a good grade. I learned a lot, especially about the diseases. The most important thing I learned, however, was how to handle long-term projects through proper time management. After all, I did the project over the course of two weeks and got it in right on time.

Recently, I told Mom, "In school, getting homework over the weekend used to be a special occasion." She replied, "Now not getting homework over the weekend is a special occasion!"

What is really important to remember, though, is that when you work hard, it pays off.

LESSON 8
You won't be perfect at everything, not even the things you do best

IN THE THIRD AND FOURTH GRADES, I was obsessed with receiving perfect marks. Well, maybe not perfect grades, just A's and B's. If I got even a smidgen less than 80 percent on a test, I would freak out and act like my world was over. The frustrating thing was that I was smart, but being an autistic kid in a mainstream school made it difficult for me to do some of the work. While I shined in language arts, math was tricky for me. I still felt that being smart was my biggest strength, and I wanted to do as well as I could possibly could, if not better, so I had trouble accepting not being perfect at school.

But one day, when I was having some difficulty with work I was doing, I had this awesome teacher tell me, "Now, Jenny, wouldn't life be really boring if you were good at everything?" I didn't think too much about it. Well, I did, but mostly in the terms of "Don't these people who are good at everything have a lot going for them?" She told me that everyone has rough times and that the important thing is that I'm doing my best.

History is chock-full of great minds failing before they succeed. Walt Disney (of all people) was once fired from a newspaper for not being "creative enough." Albert Einstein struggled in school. There's even some speculation about him having a learning disability, like autism. So I have tried to keep in mind that there will always be shortcomings and imperfections along the way.

Later in my school years, I took bad grades relatively well. A little too well in high school, because the schoolwork wasn't really helping me prepare for college and it was easy for me to fall behind. And in college, though my first semester GPA wasn't very good, I was able to cope with it. Oh well, considering high school was too easy, and the first semester of college is difficult for everyone, and the fact that I was struggling with a reading disability, it's amazing I did as well as I did!

In fan fiction, there's a word for people who are good at everything, like singing and playing musical instruments, all while looking incredibly cool and graceful. They are called "Mary Sues," in reference to a *Star Trek* fanfic story featuring a character like that. They're supposed to have fun and exciting lives too, so it's mainly the readers who get bored, not these characters. But that's another story.

LESSON 9
Mean girls aren't really popular; nice ones are

WHEN I WAS A LITTLE, whenever the word "popular girl" came to my mind, I thought of a pretty, stylish, trendy blonde cheerleader who was also catty and mean. Popular media seemed to bombard me with this message, especially movies and shows like *Mean Girls* and *Family Guy*. (Connie D'Amico, I'm looking at you.)

However, in the sixth grade, I learned that the stereotype is not always true. I had difficulty at school making friends that year due to my autism and being shy. In addition, like many other autistic kids, I had a poor sense of direction, so I had difficulty getting from class to class and often got lost. To combat this problem, Mom and the teachers decided to recruit the most popular girls from my grade to walk me from one class to the next. Mom claimed that they were cool because they were nice enough to care about special needs girls like me. I was surprised, as I had already seen enough movies and TV shows featuring popular girls who were mean. But I did appreciate what these girls did for me. And to thank them, we even had a big party together!

I started to think that I would never have to deal with mean girls at school. Autistic kids are sometimes bullied because we can be socially unaware and don't realize there are bullies out there. In high school, though, I *did* have a big issue with one girl named Mindy. (Name changed to protect the obnoxious.) Mindy would make life miserable for me. She fit my earlier "mean girl" concept well, though she wasn't blonde and wasn't a cheerleader. (My school didn't have much of a cheerleading squad.) It didn't take long for her to be nasty to me. All I had to do was ask her the weather and she would call me stupid. Once she even "jokingly" threatened to hit me. I was very upset by this, especially since she was the pretty and popular girl who was involved in many activities. She even had some of the teachers wrapped around her finger! Bullies often do that; otherwise, teachers wouldn't let them get away with their bullying.

I tried to ignore her behavior, but it became a big issue in my life. My Spanish teacher at the time, whom I admired, tried to offset the negativity by saying positive things about me while we went for a walk. He told me I was smart, funny, nice, and an expert on contemporary and classic pop culture. (One of the characters in the DeviantArt parody story I wrote around that time was based on Zorro.)

However, it wasn't all bad. I had friends too. In fact, more friends than Mindy. Her "friends" were friendly to her only because they were scared of her—they were worried that she would be mean to them—whereas my friends were friendly to me because they liked me.

After I graduated from high school and returned to the summer camp I'd attended as an intern, I saw that all my old friends from previous years welcomed me back and were sincerely happy to see me. Mom and Dad even wrote to me: "It all goes to show that the mean girls aren't really popular—you are!"

Well said, Mom and Dad. Well said.

LESSON 10
There is more to success than being popular

WHEN YOU'RE YOUNG, you think popular kids have everything: good looks, lots of company, and endless partying. Now, they probably had to manipulate and exclude a lot of people to get where they are, but that's a small price to pay, isn't it?

Well, Mindy, the girl who picked on me, wanted to make it look like she was good at everything. She played multiple sports and was even in the school band, playing guitar as well as singing. She also claimed that she had done modeling and acting. I later learned that by "acting" she meant being an extra for the Disney Channel.

When I first heard about this last thing, I was super envious. "Not fair, Mindy gets to be on Disney Channel!" I told Mom and Dad. "But Jenny, your work on DeviantArt is creative, and it has your name on it," replied Dad. My parents advised me to think more about my own accomplishments in the arts (my writing), helping the environment (making a poster about saving electricity), and athletics (swimming). I learned that as long as I focus on my own dreams, I can become successful. As Dad told me, "You can become a celebrity, not like the Kardashians who have accomplished zilch, but a celebrity like William Shakespeare. He really accomplished something worthwhile. That's why we're still reading his plays!"

LESSON 11
Don't worry about what others say

Calling somebody else fat won't make you any skinnier. Calling someone stupid doesn't make you any smarter. All you can do in life is try to solve the problem in front of you.

—Cady, played by Lindsay Lohan in *Mean Girls*

WHO KNEW LINDSAY LOHAN could give such good advice? Speaking of mean girls, around the time Mindy was picking on me, I contacted this wonderful anti-bullying blog called *Mean Stinks* about my issue with her. I wrote,

> I need help. There's a girl at school who not only picks on me no matter what I do, but seems to be good at everything and everyone seems to love her. It aggravates me too much, even though it shouldn't, and another girl is friends with her and is moody to pretty much everyone else, including me. We used to be friends until she came along. How can I stop getting angry around her?

They replied with wonderful comments, like "What she says and does doesn't mean anything, and you are beautiful, Jennifer." They also had many good anti-bullying suggestions on the blog, including writing positive notes to my friends (which I continue to do), such as "You're worth it" and "Everything's going to be great." I even wrote Mindy a card, which she didn't appreciate, but everything else helped me cope with her bullying.

There was also a girl, Maureen, who hated everything I did and got mad at me if I said anything she considered even remotely offensive. (Name changed to protect the perpetually offended.) For instance, when I made up silly parodies of the infamous Rebecca Black song, "Friday," she was offended because Friday was the day of her dance recital. I wasn't saying anything insulting about Fridays; in fact, my song was Friday-positive. But she still got angry.

Mindy had Maureen wrapped around her finger, so Maureen sometimes tried to defend her by saying that my annoying jokes motivated her to bully me. In other words, that I somehow "deserved" it. Often when kids are bullied, the victim is blamed, especially when the victim is autistic.

Even after Mindy left our high school, I was still upset about her. I was also having trouble with the Girls' Group at school, which was supposed to be a support group. Instead, the other girls kept saying negative things about me. Ironically, this group included the school "feminist," Ira. (Name changed to protect an ideological phony.) Whatever happened to women using female empowerment to look out for each other?

All this bullying was upsetting, but Mom reassured me that a lot of girls are mean in high school and that what they say isn't important in the long run. It took me a long time, but I learned that you shouldn't care about mean comments. Instead, you should look at actions. Once, when I told Maureen that Mindy was (read: claimed to be) an extra on a TV show, she said, "She's out there doing stuff, unlike you," trying to hurt me. Yeah, being a TV extra (i.e., a piece of scenery) is obviously a lot more important than my work collecting jeans, school supplies, and canned food for kids in poverty. Unlike Mindy, I was trying to help people, and I was putting effort into my projects. I now know that that's what really matters.

Oh, and by the way, thanks for the support, *Mean Stinks*!

PART III
FRIENDS AND FAMILY

LESSON 12
Be open to everyone

EVERY NEW YEAR'S EVE, my family used to have a little mini-party at our local diner with other special needs families. While most of us had fun, there were some kids who were overwhelmed by the unfamiliar setting. So Mom and Dad decided it would be better to throw New Year's parties for special needs families at our home. Mom would cook up a huge bowl of chili (gluten-free), and everyone else would contribute to a potluck dinner.

While I liked the idea, I wondered whether a party for special needs kids would be "reverse discrimination." Mom and Dad reassured me that it was "affirmative action," because we were helping families find respite over the New Year when they have to deal with their special needs children. Of course their "normal" siblings would be welcome too.

I decided to give the party a nineties theme, complete with a playlist of cheesy pop and rock music. I even taped a nineties movie, *Why Do Fools Fall in Love?* As I looked around the living room while all the kids were watching the movie and eating munchies together, I thought to myself, *We have all the bases covered. We have the high-functioning kids, the Asperger's kids, the PDD kids, an autistic prodigy, the classic autism kids, and even their neurotypical siblings. Good job, Mom and Dad.*

While I can't connect with every autistic kid, I still believe that this kind of inclusion is a great idea. I actually had a friend with Asperger's who wanted to come to the party but stayed away because he gets frustrated around low-functioning kids. At least I can handle that. After all, the more autistic you are, the fewer places there are for you on New Year's Eve. You should welcome everyone to your home, regardless of their condition.

LESSON 13
Not everyone can take a joke (and some jokes aren't funny)

IN THE ELEVENTH GRADE, there was a boy in my class who liked to pick on me. He would go out of his way to annoy me. One time, for instance, he stole the Batman toy I had with my Robin costume at the school Halloween party. Since he reminded me of Edward from *Twilight*, I jokingly said to him, "Hi, Edward, how's Bella?" He didn't exactly appreciate the joke. Being a sparkly vampire wasn't the image he wanted to project. The fact that my other friends, like Elle, would join in to poke fun at him didn't help much. For example, after I mentioned to her how much he reminded me of Edward, Elle jokingly asked him to "bite [her]." (Name changed to protect a smart-mouth.)

As the school year progressed, the jokes became more frequent and (to him) more annoying. I was bored at school, so I felt I needed a fantasy romance like the one *Twilight's* Bella had. I didn't even really have a crush on him, I just needed some fantasy in my life. Once, for example, he was watching a movie on his iPad, and I joked that he was watching *Eclipse*, one of the Twilight movies. My teacher was not too happy about that, as I was repeating it for the sixtieth time and the other girls were annoyed at my behavior.

Now I realize that while these jokes may be funny to me, they aren't always so funny to others, especially to those who are oversensitive, the target of the joke, or both. And I realize that most teenage boys hate *Twilight*.

LESSON 14
Make your own choices

IN THE SUMMER BEFORE THE FIFTH GRADE, my fourth-grade teacher Miss Rossi was having yoga lessons at my day camp. (Name changed to protect the incredibly cute.) While Miss Rossi was a wonderful teacher, I was more interested in girly activities like beading jewelry, so I never signed up for the class. At the very end of camp, Mom asked, "Jenny, did you see Miss Rossi at all this summer?" I wanted to tell Mom I was more interested in the other activities, but didn't know how. I didn't attend her lessons simply because I wanted to do other things, but I was too shy to say so.

In the eighth grade, a really cool guy named Lance came to school and automatically decided he wanted to be my friend. (Name changed to protect the hip.) Now Lance has really interesting tastes in movies, TV, music, and clothes. He enjoys the Madea films, he likes shows like *Cops*, his favorite music is EDM (electronic dance music), and he loves Abercrombie & Fitch clothes. He wanted me to be interested in those things too. While there was some overlap—I did like Abercrombie & Fitch, for instance—there were also some differences. I didn't care much for EDM.

We talked about this one day in our Girls' Group at school, and one of the girls told me, "Jenny, you don't have to have Lance tell you what to do all the time. You can think for yourself and choose what you like."

At first I didn't know how to take the advice. I've let other people dictate my tastes for most of my life, as I was never really sure about my identity. But I now understand that the only person who can really decide what I like is me. Just because your friends all like the same movie, book, or food, doesn't mean you have to like that as well. The important thing is to be yourself and do what you actually like.

LESSON 15
It's okay to say "no" to a friend

WHILE I WAS TRYING TO ADJUST to my high school, there was a neighborhood girl who would visit me named Victoria (another fictitious name). Victoria always insisted that I play with her whenever she came over. Thing is, I was usually exhausted by the end of the day. For example, one day I had school and a doctor's appointment, then Victoria came over, and since I couldn't say "no," she took over the rest of my afternoon, and then it was time to go to Temple Youth Group. I got really upset due to my lack of downtime, but one of my mom's friends calmed me down.

In 2011, during spring break, my good friends Kurt (Lesson 4) and Lance (Lesson 14) invited me to come with them to an indoor water park, but I was feeling under the weather. I had a doctor's appointment that morning, and I didn't want to do too much in one day. I also wanted to enjoy myself during spring break, but Mom and Dad advised me to stay home. I was a bit skeptical about it at first, but then decided to listen to them. So I spent most of the afternoon relaxing in the basement and reading magazines while listening to the Beatles. It was the right choice for me, since I would have found the water park overwhelming in that state of exhaustion.

What I've learned from this episode is that you can't always say "yes" to a friend, even if you feel like you should. You have to listen to yourself, too (and sometimes your parents).

LESSON 16
Mom is glamorous, even if she's not Jenny McCarthy-glamorous

WHEN I WAS ELEVEN, my mom met Jenny McCarthy, and I'll never forget what she said about her: "She's a blonde bombshell, and she's still done a lot for our cause!" Jenny McCarthy reminds me of the mom from *American Dad*, Francine, who's also a self-admitted blonde bombshell, but is "pretty smart when she's had her eight hours!" I was incredibly envious of her son, Evan, because he had a "glam mom." I didn't even care about the media attention she got, positive or negative, because to me, she was the epitome of glamorous. I talked all the time about getting her to "adopt me."

Then, in April 2008, I finally got to meet her at an AutismOne conference Mom dragged me to. She said, "Hi, cutie!" and autographed my book while we got our picture taken. Thanks, Jenny!

At the conference, she talked about how autism moms shouldn't be seen as bad parents just because their kids are autistic. There were a lot more dads attending the conference where she spoke, for an obvious reason. As Jenny and Mom said to each other, "Whatever works!" The conferences were usually more popular with moms than dads, and Mom and Jenny needed as much support as they could get. I call these dads Jenny's Testosterone Brigade. Even better, Jenny told these dads that they would be "rewarded" by their wives, if you catch my drift.

When my grandma heard that I had met Jenny, she asked me a bunch of questions. Among them was: "Did Jenny McCarthy adopt you?" Of course, all I got was her autograph. It's not like she had the time and energy for another special needs child.

Now I know that while Jenny has worked wonders for our cause, she's not the only autism mom out there who deserves recognition. There are also other autism moms, like mine, who aren't supermodels but are still incredible. In fact, Jenny McCarthy once signed and gave me a certificate saying my mom was a "glam mom"!

Others also agree with this. When I was at the doctor's office and asked the nurse why my mom was cool, she said, "Well, she has great taste in clothes!" referring to Mom's stylish jeans, along with, "She's an advocate for many things." All autism moms are glamorous in their own way because they work hard for their kids.

LESSON 17
Little sisters show empathy in their own ways

WHEN YOU'RE A TEENAGER, you have a lot of issues to deal with, whether you're autistic or typical. I had to deal with a little sister named Flora who was very sensitive. Despite being a "tween," she had the mentality of a much younger child, which is pretty much the norm for kids with lower-functioning autism. She would get upset whenever I got even remotely upset. If I raised my voice a few decibels (well, maybe more than a few), she became super emotional. Sometimes I felt like I couldn't express my true feelings without her losing it.

For example, one time before a shopping date with a friend, I was reading the Internet for clothing ideas. (I was going through something of a bubblegum-goth phase.) Unfortunately, the computer was misbehaving and shut down spontaneously. I got pretty upset, and Flora flew off the handle. In hindsight, I now realize that I should have controlled my feelings better.

There's an interesting story behind her attitude toward my feelings. Back when I was in the sixth grade, Mom and Dad told me that my school might not be right for me. I was devastated when they said that over dinner, because as hard as it was for me there, I did enjoy that school on some level. Plus, moving to another school would put yet another problem on my plate. Then Flora did a beautiful thing: she dried my tears and pushed up the corners of my mouth to make me smile! It was like a ray of light in this dark situation.

This is why whenever I get upset, my sister gets upset too. It's her own little way of showing empathy. Considering that autistic kids have difficulty showing empathy, this is very sweet of her, even if she tries too hard sometimes.

LESSON 18
Learn to take jokes,
even your dad's

MY DAD, LIKE ANY FATHER of a teenage girl, has lots of dumb jokes up his sleeve. He makes fun of the music I like by grooving to it, and he points out that Iron Man needs a can opener to change his underwear. Unfortunately, when you have a literal mind like I do, you can be very easily put off by some of these jokes.

For example, when I was twelve, our Internet service crashed. Because I was obsessed with my computer at the time, I was devastated. I was a complete drama queen, even going as far as faking my own death by falling to the floor and pretending not to move. Dad joked, "All the electricity is going off. We're going back to the age of fire!" Because I was already in a bad mood, I was very offended by what he said, because I *really* wanted to get online. Mom reassured me that he was joking, but I was still angry at him.

His "jokes" continued. When the Lady Gaga song "Bad Romance" was popular, he sang the line "you and me can write a bad romance" as "you and me can write a bad pop song!" I was mad: "How would you feel if I made fun of the music you liked, Dad?"

I could have tried to make fun of the older bands I knew. Unfortunately, while Dad was old enough to remember bands and musicians like the Beatles, the Rolling Stones, the Doors, Elvis, Queen, Steve Miller Band, and others, that doesn't mean he liked them enough to get upset. He was a nerd and not really into rock music. So making fun of them was pointless. As he said, "Oh, I wouldn't mind!"

My dad still makes up a lot of "dumb daddy jokes," as my mom likes to call them. One time, when the TV broke down, he read the instructions in Spanish. He noticed that the Spanish for "remote control" is *el control remoto*. So now, whenever I listen to "Spanglish" songs on the radio, he sings about *el control remoto*. He says, "It sounds so beautiful in Spanish."

I've learned to cope with these by now. Even if you don't like your parents' sense of humor, you should at least realize it's all in good fun. And if you listen to the jokes with an open mind, you might eventually have to admit they can be pretty funny.

Also, jokes in general can be a great way to get through life and problems. For example, at my very first birthday party, my grandpa leaned over and said, "Well, Jenny, another year shot to hell." That's become our family motto: we even put it on our holiday cards!

PART IV
AUTISM

LESSON 19
You're different, and that's okay

Mom always tells me to celebrate everyone's uniqueness. I like the way that sounds.

—Hilary Duff

WHILE MOM AND DAD ARE CERTAIN that I will graduate from college, hold a job, get married, and eventually have children, they also know I will be different from other people.

I always knew I was different. That's what being one of the only special needs kid at your school for most of your childhood does to you. But I rarely thought of myself as autistic. I wanted to do what normal kids did, like have sleepovers and join Girl Scouts. Girl Scouts worked out horribly for me, but that's another story. ("Don't worry about it, Jenny," my dad told me. "I only lasted a year in the Cub Scouts. Then I was court-martialed.")

Now I realize that regardless of how "normal" I try to be, autism will always be a part of me. Not all of me, but still a part of me. But as Miss Montana 2012 Alexis Wineman says, "Autism doesn't define me, I define autism!"

Fortunately, for the most part, people have accepted me despite my differences. In the sixth grade, for example, I had difficulty finding my way around the building (autism can do that to you), so other girls helped me. I would joke with them about the part of

Horton Hears a Who! (one of my favorite movies) where the puff-ball, Katie, says, "In my world, everyone's a pony, and they all eat rainbows and poop butterflies!" While these jokes were immature for eleven-year-olds, the girls still joked around with me.

There are some other ways I might stand out. I dress somewhat different with my own style, for example—big men's shirts with jeans. I also have unconventional tastes in entertainment (for a teenager), as I like classic rock and classic movies.

But being different isn't necessarily a bad thing. Yes, there are negatives, but as long as I don't get upset, or obsess, I'm fine. While I understand why helping kids with autism recover is necessary, I also understand some autistic people don't want to be cured. That's also okay. Mom once told me, "You have the right kind of autism. You think outside the box." In fact, a lot of creative minds, from Tim Burton to Michael Jackson, may have had autism. While I would have been smart with or without autism, I've used my obsessions constructively.

I may be a quirky person, but that's okay. It's part of who I am.

LESSON 20
But sometimes you have to try to fit in

OF COURSE, THERE ARE ALSO some things to watch out for. In middle school, for instance, I felt very stressed dealing with a highly structured learning environment. I would often get upset, like when I accidentally left my planner at home. My mom had to remind me several times that my meltdowns would alienate me from other people. And hearing that would stress me even more.

Back then, I saw a musical called *Grease*, which was about a sweetheart who turned into a bad girl to impress a boy and his friends. Mom thought that while the musical was fun, the girl was fine just the way she was, and she shouldn't have felt that she had to conform to the other bad girls. To be fair, moms are always telling you, "Just be yourself." And, of course, the girl was pretty cute to begin with, so the transformation hardly seemed necessary. Also, my mom's a mom, so of course she would think like that. She's also a nerd, so she would relate to characters who were "different."

I was really interested in this question of fitting in, however. *Grease* was basically saying that conformity is good, so I discussed that idea with Mom.

"Now," she said, "having different interests from your friends, like movies, is fine. But if you get upset too much, you won't have many friends. In that sense, you have to conform."

So sometimes it makes sense to match the behavior of others around me. For example, I threw a party for the girls who had helped me from class to class, like a "typical" girl would. Mom helped me to adapt my behavior in other ways as well. For example, if I was good at controlling my emotions all week, I would get a movie. It took a little while, but I finally learned how to control myself. In fact, when some girls from middle school saw me several years later, they were very impressed at how much I had changed!

LESSON 21
It's easier to make friends with people you can relate to

UNTIL THE EIGHTH GRADE, I didn't have a lot of friends. When I did have friends, they were either a lot older (like some of the teachers) or a lot younger (like the kids and grandkids of my neighbors). I didn't really understand the concept of friends, so I didn't realize what I was missing. At least not that much, as I did once hear Mom say, "Jenny is closer to kids younger than her than kids her age."

There was an autistic boy in my school who bothered me by reading slowly. I would get very upset at him, but Mom assured me that I was doing that because I felt I was being rejected and wanted to reject others before I could be rejected again. So I tried to find some common ground with him instead. I found out that this boy liked *South Park*. Because my favorite musician at the time was Kanye West, I showed the boy a picture of the *South Park* episode that made fun of Kanye West. He thought it was funny, and the next day I tried to joke with him about it. However, the teacher told me it was inappropriate, and I got upset. True, everything in *South Park* is inappropriate, but that's the whole point of the program. It's eighth-grade humor, so can you blame eighth-graders for liking it?

Anyway, I built up a steady friendship with this boy over the summer. We went to amusement parks and a museum. I learned that he liked to joke about Selena Gomez, cellos, and *Jersey Shore*. Some neurotypical kids might have thought that it was weird that he was obsessing over the same topics, and there was even a girl at school who was also autistic, but still hated his jokes. Yet, I could relate to him because we shared similar interests.

A few years later, my dad saw an online article about how some kids with special needs work better in alternative schools than public schools. He wrote in a comment that my sister was too seriously affected to be mainstreamed, but that for me, mainstreaming had worked in the lower grades. Mom said, "Well, that's because autistic people connect better with other autistic people." I pointed out that most mainstream schools, like my sister's high school, have separate classrooms for low-functioning and neurotypical kids, but they can't really handle those in the middle, with high-functioning autism or Asperger's—like me. We don't need a separate classroom, but we sometimes have difficulty functioning in a mainstream one, because it can be harder to find those we can relate to there.

I learned that when I'm with people who are more like me, I feel more comfortable, and it's easier for me to make friends. However, that doesn't mean that I can't make friends in the "mainstream" world. I'm going to college, where I am making both neurotypical and autistic friends. I belong to an anime club, where we sit around watching and discussing popular Japanese animation. While it's not uncommon for kids with high-functioning autism to have unconventional entertainment tastes, not all anime fans are on the spectrum. Both autistic and neurotypical kids like to talk about anime trivia, and that gives us a common bond.

You can make friends of all backgrounds; the important thing is that you share pastimes and passions.

LESSON 22
Rated "O" for "Obsessive"

ONE OF THE THINGS THAT can make it harder to relate to people is that high-functioning autistic kids like me often have very narrow interests, like train schedules. Mine was film ratings. Yeah, yeah, it sounds weird, but it's true. I call these interests "mechanical" interests, because autistic kids are drawn to all sorts of technology-related topics. For example, I once saw an autistic boy watching the gears of a bubble-making machine as if it were a movie. Sometimes I would talk about my mechanical interests when I should have been focusing on more immediate things, like preparing to go to school. I would spend hours on Wikipedia looking up the film rating systems of various countries.

Looking back, I feel kind of bad for obsessing over these topics. After all, the people who make the film ratings aren't very popular, as many fans associate them with censorship. (They say MPAA stands for Mindless People Advocating Awfulness).

Furthermore, I was doing HBOT at the time. (That's our Hyperbaric Oxygen Treatment chamber, which helps heal the brain. It's also very relaxing, like a space capsule.) People tend to remember what they read, watch, or listen to in HBOT, because when you're in the chamber the rest of the world is completely shut out. I spent a lot of time in HBOT with a DVD player watching cartoons. My two favorite cartoons when I was ten were *Veggie Tales* and *The Simpsons,* and I was quite obsessive about both.

I talked constantly about the shows with my parents, until they said, "You can talk about anything you want, as long as it isn't about *Veggie Tales*." (By the way, I'm not saying anything bad about HBOT. It can be very beneficial for individuals with autism and similar disorders. In fact, Michael Jackson had one! It just had the side effect of making me obsess about topics. You know, bringing my inner thoughts to the surface.)

Now I know that I should expand my interests so that other people can enjoy what I like with me. Kids on the autism spectrum can often obsess over certain topics, or get upset, or be shy, but we can work at overcoming these behaviors, and we can occasionally have "normal" thoughts (for example, whenever the voice in our head calls us out for our misbehavior).

LESSON 23
Think for yourself when it comes to autism

IN THE AUTISM COMMUNITY, there's a "neurodiversity" movement that basically sends the message that autistic people are just like you and me. This may sound like a good idea for some people—and it is, to some degree, as autistic people who are intelligent and high-functioning enough obviously don't need a cure. However, it isn't fair to autistic kids who struggle with life and can't do things the rest of us take for granted, like speaking. I'm recovering from autism, and people who tell me that I shouldn't recover—that autism is just another way of thinking—aren't very helpful, because they ignore the issues autistic kids face every day.

Not long ago, I made a video called "We beat autism!" and posted it on YouTube. Mom and Dad thought it was ingenious, but I was worried about how the neurodiversity activists would take it.

While most of the feedback to my video was positive, there was one girl who said, "You can't separate yourself from your autism, dear." Now, I am still technically on the autism spectrum, but I've still come a long way from when I was a kid. In fact, Mom and Dad say that without the treatments they did for me, I wouldn't be going to college. Unfortunately, many kids in college who are autistic don't make it past the first semester, even with accommodations.

Of course, at the end of the day, that girl's comments didn't matter. I decided to ignore them and just focus on talking about my recovery. At the end of the day, you need to think for yourself and do what's best for you.

Flora and I: computer jockettes.

The whole family wearing my official bat mitzvah sweatshirt ("Friend of Jenny").

My friends and I at summer camp.

On horseback at summer camp (not exactly the Lone Ranger).

Dancing the hora at my bat mitzvah.

When I was little, my dad would stand me on the bathroom sink, and we'd stick out our tongues at the mirror. We still have fun together!

With my boyfriend, Matt.

Flora and I dolled up for Valentine's Day.

We're the first generation in history that actually likes our parents' music!

Studying for my bat mitzvah with my excellent tutor, Bonnie.

Mutual admiration: Jenny and Jenny (McCarthy and Rose).

Another tree-hugging
environmentalist!

Flora and I in the car.

At college and on my own. Made it after all!

LESSON 24
Autism work isn't always glamorous

IN OCTOBER 2012, THE MEDIA was very excited to share the story of Katy Perry singing with autistic musician Jodi DiPiazza. A lot of people, including Jon Stewart, were also thrilled. But not my mom. She pointed out that my sister is also an autistic singer, but she doesn't get attention like that. I thought, "Well, Katy Perry's music will draw people, and she's helping this girl feel good about herself, what's wrong with that?" The point is, very few autistic kids are as lucky as Jodi is. Most kids, let alone autistic kids, don't get to be on TV with their favorite pop stars.

In April 2014, I published an article about this issue in the online newspaper *Age of Autism*. Even though it's wonderful for autistic kids to shine with celebrities, I wrote, most of them will not be that lucky. Some can't speak, and others wander from home. The comments I got for the article were overwhelmingly positive, from a man who said I did a wonderful job of highlighting everyday autism to a girl who said I spoke for so many autistic kids.

Later that year, my dad was reading a story online about how the more "real-life" autism work isn't taken seriously. There was even a little box included with the story that said, "If you want stuff sugar-coated, I advise that you visit a bakery." One of the commentators was a mom who was angry at the fact that only talented autistic kids got public attention.

I talked about it with Dad, and he explained, "Well, Jenny, if we only do photo ops with celebrities, we accomplish nothing." While it's great to celebrate the talents of autistic kids (more on that in the next lesson), you also have to deal with the hard issue of autism itself and its less pretty features.

That's not to say autism work can't be fun and glamorous. Just ask Alexis Wineman, Jenny McCarthy, or Jacqueline Laurita. It just can't be like that all the time. It's like chocolate—I like it, but I can't eat it at every meal! And come to think of it, even unglamorous autism work can be fun and beautiful in its own little way. For example, I didn't get very famous through the fantasy story I wrote with the boy from my school, but we had a good time writing it. And it meant so much to him.

Celebrate autistic kids without celebrating autism

THE MAINSTREAM MEDIA often has a lot of sweet stories about autism, from little girls singing with Katy Perry to young women becoming beauty queens. They're nice, but the media sometimes acts like it was autism that gave them special talents. While some autistic people credit their autism with helping them think outside the box, not every autistic kid will be a cute kid with special talents.

For example, back in 2011, an autistic girl at my school, Elizabeth Bonker, published a book of poetry. She got a lot of attention for the book, and the school's website pointed out that autistic children "found their voice" through the arts. Yes, some autistic kids can express themselves through creative work. When I was ten years old and not talking very much, I wrote. In fact, I founded, wrote, and edited my own newspaper called *The Backpack News*!

Sometimes the media likes to showcase autistic kids who have special talents, but we can't forget about the autistic kids who aren't so gifted. Stories like this are often used to suggest that "autism isn't so bad," even though the autism rate has risen so much in recent years.

I was afraid that some writers for autism blogs would dismiss this poetry book as a shallow fluff story about how wonderful autism is, because they understand that autism is very difficult for most kids. After all, some parents want to bring to light the issues their kids face every day, and their kids can't connect with a kid who makes a three-pointer in basketball or a little girl who paints pretty pictures. However, they were fascinated by the book, because they could relate to it, as their kids were feeling what Elizabeth wrote about in her poetry. The book itself did not say "autism is good"; quite the opposite. Elizabeth wanted to speak, but couldn't, so she typed to express her true feelings. The book has also received praise from many famous activists with varying views on autism, from Temple Grandin to Jenny McCarthy. Basically, Elizabeth's mom had her write the book to show how much autistic kids are hiding and have to offer. In fact, Elizabeth was tested twice: the first test indicated that she was delayed, but after she learned to communicate, the second test showed that she was very intelligent. In other words, she was hiding so much talent behind her autism!

You should celebrate an autistic kid's accomplishments, but you shouldn't really celebrate a disability. When we celebrate the achievements of Franklin D. Roosevelt, we celebrate the great things he did *despite* having polio. We don't celebrate polio itself. After all, when we celebrate a disability, we forget the burdens it imposes on people.

PART V
OPTIMISM

LESSON 26
Down times will be bouncing up soon . . .

An arrow can only be shot by pulling it backward. So when life is dragging you back with difficulties, it means that it's going to launch you into something great.

—Unknown

IN THE EIGHTH GRADE, I didn't have an easy time. In fact, it was awful for me. It all started in late August when my grandpa's health started failing and went downhill from there. Okay, so technically I had issues beforehand, and it's not as if all the positivity in my life came to a screeching halt, but there were a lot of factors that ruined my thirteenth year. I didn't always handle these all that well. If I didn't get what I wanted, I would spin out of control and start crying. I even had to leave school early several times for "behavioral issues."

Some of the difficulties were caused by the school building's renovation, which stirred up my allergies. I was mostly nasty at school. At home, Hebrew tutoring, and other activities, I was fine. I was also busy studying for my bat mitzvah, and while that was fun, the stress my family and I were going through was not . . . and it didn't end when I finished reading my Torah portion. Over the next month, my parents had to look for another school, as my current school didn't know how to handle my behavior. I narrowly missed the Honor Roll. This was a big deal, as I normally got A's and B's.

I wanted to do the school play, but I couldn't because of my emotional outbursts.

At my next school, everything seemed to be fine for a while. I was making friends and jokes about Tiger Woods. But by January I fell apart. I got upset at another student and was sentenced to an in-school suspension the next day. That day I tried to stay calm, but it didn't work. I lost it. Mom and Dad came to pick me up, and I was suspended for two weeks.

That's when Mom and Dad saw the light and sent me to a third school, which turned out to be awesome. It was very chill, as it was founded in 1970 by hippies. There were a lot of fun activities for me to explore my creativity and help boost my dreams—fashion design, music class, acting. I was going through a pop music phase and wanted to be like my idols at the time, Avril Lavigne and Hilary Duff, who were also involved in acting and fashion design. However, even there I was getting upset and feeling hopeless. Even little things seemed to set me off, like a boy reading too slowly.

But my life really perked up in the ninth grade. In her Christmas letters, Mom wrote, "From time to time, we have to retrieve letters Jenny put in the mail. She's sending wrinkled-up dollar bills to charities." Mom was surprised—and impressed!—that I cared for people I had never met. I was finally becoming more aware of my surroundings, and donating to help organizations like the Brain Injury Association of Minnesota and Eat So They Can reflected this. I also had some close friends for the first time since elementary school.

But the best part of the ninth grade was going to the Rally to Restore Sanity in Washington. I love Jon Stewart, and even though the rally itself was insane with all the people there, the basic message of lots of people coming together to save American society was beautiful. Kid Rock and Sheryl Crow did a wonderful song called "Care" to show that even though we can't to put a bandage on the world's problems, that doesn't mean we're not concerned. And the night after the rally I found my "Kids Celebrate America" CD, which I used to play when I was younger. It was a great nostalgia trip. The kids' version of "Imagine" was beautiful, as it showed how I was exposed to wonderful music, like John Lennon, at an early age.

So you see, even if you feel you've hit rock bottom, you've actually started to bounce back, and you never know what little thing might set you on the happier track.

LESSON 27
... meanwhile, enjoy what you have

THERE WAS ONE DAY WHEN I spun out of control at school. Another student was reading slowly, and I got mad at him because I wanted him to catch up, so I started screaming. When Mom and Dad asked about it, I refused to speak about it and got more upset. Mom said I should put more focus on being a happier person, so I made a list on her computer called "100 Reasons to Be Happy." Now, that was a big deal considering how upset I felt at the time. At first, I didn't think I could find thirteen reasons—I was thirteen years old at the time—let alone a hundred. But I did it anyway! Most were rather silly, some were sweet, but the important thing was that I had made an effort to find reasons to be happy, and it actually made a difference.

By the way, I know some of them aren't so great. I was thirteen when I wrote them, okay? I've kept the original spelling and grammar.

Observe:

100. Mom is getting contacts to look prettier.
 99. Pretty much everything happens for a reason.
 98. I am sweet enough to make a CD for my mom.
 97. My totally awesome Backyard Sports movie.
 96. I am going to be a singer soon.
 95. Who knows, I just may have my own clothing line too!

94. My doctor is my "third parent," and he's a cool guy to talk to.

93. I've gotten through my thirteenth (fourteenth?) year.

92. If I can get through that, I can get through anything.

91. I'll be getting my ears pierced in a year.

90. And I've gotten used to shots thanks to chelation.

89. I'll be getting my driver's license in two and a half years. *(As this book goes to press, I have yet to get my driver's license.)*

88. Two words: Kanye West.

87. Another two words: John Hodgman.

86. I need another two words!

85. And I'm almost finished with John Hodgman's second book.

84. But I haven't read his first one.

83. Or *Diary of a Wimpy Kid: Dog Days*.

82. John Hodgman is writing a third book!

81. Looking at Doctor Who pictures while listening to my favorite songs.

80. There are Doctor Who episodes for me to watch.

79. He's so cute!

78. Okay, maybe not the first nine Doctor Whos, but the latest two are adorable.

77. And then there are those cool songs.

76. My little sister is going to make Kidz Bop-style CDs for special needs children soon.

75. And they'll be cooler than Kidz Bop, cause she'll be the only one singing.

74. I'm trying to make several of my dreams come true.

73. Cause I'm the kinda girl who makes her dreams come true.

72. And I'll be a great role model for young girls once I become famous!

71. I'm breaking the mold by writing my own movies.

70. Uncyclopedia is funny.

69. Great food from the school cafeteria.

68. So many kids would be jealous of me and all.

67. How could I live without sushi?

66. *Diary of a Wimpy Kid.*

65. *Diary of a Wimpy Kid: Rodrick Rules.*

64. *Diary of a Wimpy Kid: The Last Straw.*
63. *Diary of a Wimpy Kid: The Movie Diary.*
62. *Diary of a Wimpy Kid Do-It-Yourself book.*
61. And *Diary of a Wimpy Kid: The Movie!*
60. Plus, there's seventh book on the horizon.
59. I sent a letter to Kanye West.
58. I still haven't heard from him, so there's a chance his response will be good.
57. The chef at my school cafeteria is Italian.
56. My little sister is so cute.
55. And funny.
54. And she seems to be getting better every day.
53. So am I.
52. Pizza on Tuesday nights.
51. Mom loves me.
50. Dad loves me.
49. And Flora loves me!
48. And I'm pretty sure Elmo loves me too.
47. My sister has a favorite Jonas Brother: she's acting more like a ten-year-old! Yay!
46. Flora singing songs from the radio is adorable.
45. And what she thinks about Nikki Minaj is hilarious!
44. My sister with her "toy ant colony" is adorable.
43. Roller Coaster Tycoon 3: Gold!
42. It would be fun to make up a cool theme park.
41. Sim City: Life Stories.
40. There's a game or two I haven't played yet.
39. Those games would be fun.
38. No matter what they are, I'm sure they'll be fun.
37. Playing games while listening to Itunes.
36. Our Elmo doll is adorable.
35. Whether Mom . . .
34. . . . me . . .
33. . . . or Flora is making him talk!
32. *Clarissa Explains It All.*

31. *The Daily Show with Jon Stewart*.
30. *Phineas and Ferb*.
29. This awesome Phineas and Ferb TV movie I'm writing.
28. *The Simpsons* on Sunday nights.
27. Radio 92.3 NOW.
26. *Fresh: Acoustic Sunrise* on Sunday mornings.
25. 95.5 WPLJ.
24. Commercial Free Mondays on 92.3 NOW.
23. Radio Z100.
22. Fresh 102.7.
21. Saturday night movies.
20. Saturday night *Daily Show/Phineas and Ferb* marathons.
19. Not many teenagers have developed tastes.
18. I'm unique.
17. If I can have a bat mitzvah . . .
16. . . . I can do anything!
15. I have an awesome handbag.
14. The world needs more people like me . . .
13. . . . cause I love giving people help who need it.
12. Case in point: When my sister couldn't sleep at night, I gave her a heartbeat CD . . .
11. . . . read her stories . . .
10. . . . and put Phineas and Ferb posters on the walls of her room.
9. Another case in point: My grandparents aren't feeling well, so I give them jokes . . .
8. . . . stories . . .
7. . . . and I even went out of my way to share my Ipod with them!
6. That's how considerate I am.
5. And another case in point: I have texted at least $100 to Haiti Benefits so that people can get well.
4. I need another case in point to show how considerate I am!
3. And another!
2. There are plenty of problems I can solve.
And the number one reason to be happy?
1. The "alternative" is pretty boring.

A while later, Mom found this list on her computer. She wrote a letter to Dad, saying:

"Jenny wrote this on my computer, right after she lost it.

She's going to be okay."

D'awwww.

This story reminds me of a blind author who visited my school and said, "You can last several weeks without food, several days without water, a minute without oxygen, but not four seconds without hope." That is so true. Regardless of how hopeless you feel, you're never truly hopeless, and if you try to get past how upset you feel and try to find something positive, you could probably come up with 100 things of your own.

LESSON 28
You can do anything you set your mind to

THOUGH I AM PRETTY SMART, my disability has sometimes kept me from doing as well as my classmates. For example, in music class, while others were able to play instruments like the flute well, I could not, as my fingers simply couldn't adjust to the flute. More importantly, at our temple, I had difficulty learning Hebrew. Learning a new language with an unfamiliar alphabet is hard for most children, but it is especially hard for a special needs child. I had to repeat the same words over and over again because I just couldn't understand them.

We switched to another temple, and I tried again to study for my bat mitzvah. I was already having issues with the transition from elementary school to middle school, and now I had another thing on my mind. But this time I worked with a dedicated tutor named Bonnie. (Name has not been changed—to acknowledge the wonderful.) While it was difficult at first learning the letters, I was able to do the full service by Halloween 2009, which was the day of my bat mitzvah.

Recently I was looking at my dad's computer—okay, I was spying again—and I found things he had written about me when I was ten years younger. He wrote lots of positive things, such as "She's an avid reader," "She likes to study foreign languages," and "She likes to think outside the box," which showed me that I had a lot of potential even then. But I also found a letter he had written to the director of my first Hebrew school, asking that I be excused from Hebrew lessons. He had written,

> It has become clear that her learning disability is blocking her efforts to learn the language. I've been working on it with her, but she is making no real progress: every day we have to start again at the beginning. It's becoming a source of serious frustration for her. Jenny actually does quite well in most academic subjects at school, but given her autism, we have had to face the fact that she simply can't do certain things. . . . Mastering an entirely new alphabet that is read in reverse isn't easy for anyone, but it can be particularly baffling for an autistic child. Like most kids nowadays, Jenny has to cope with a heavy load of academic and extracurricular activities, and for the most part she copes successfully. But we honestly don't want to push her into something that will only drain her energies and demoralize her.

I had completely forgotten about that letter. I remembered that we had given up on Hebrew for a while, but not the story behind it, especially since I was able to catch up later thanks to my wonderful tutor.

That night, Mom came into my room and said, "Now Jenny, did you find that letter on Dad's computer? That was when we weren't sure you were ready for Hebrew. Now look at you: you had your bat mitzvah, you're going to college, you've come a long way!"

This all goes to show that just because you may think you can't do something, that doesn't mean you'll never be able to do it. You may eventually make it happen. You can always try again.

LESSON 29
You might miss some opportunities, but there will be others

IN DECEMBER 2012, MY MOM had the ingenious idea to get kids recovering from autism to testify before Congress. Mom wanted to get our message across that recovery from autism is possible. I thought it was brilliant, partly because I would get my fifteen minutes of fame, and partly because I would get to help lots of autism families. If you asked me, "Do you want to do this to help people or to be famous?" I would have said, "Yes."

However, as awesome as it sounds, organizing something like this would take a lot of time and work. Mom tried to get something set up when she went to the AutismOne conference, which already had autism superstars Jenny McCarthy, Jacqueline Laurita (a real autism mom on *Real Housewives of New Jersey*), and Alexis Wineman. I was a little disappointed when I found out that I might have to wait all year to speak to Congress. But nothing could have prepared me for what would eventually happen.

It turned out that California Congressman Darrell Issa wanted to hold the hearings but had to cancel them for unexplained reasons, and my heart broke. Basically, recovered kids had been denied a platform to speak about autism and their experiences. I cried for a long time, though seeing Matthew Broderick on *The Daily Show* advertise pizza made me feel a little better. (He's kind of a guilty pleasure, sort of like Adam West.)

The cancellation was a setback, but I tried to think of other ideas to speak publicly about autism. In June 2014, I came up with an idea to showcase recovered kids through YouTube videos. Basically, we would talk about our experiences with autism for a minute, and then the video would fade, leaving the words "We Beat Autism!" on the screen. The project took a little planning, and it was hard to find time between summer camp work and preparing for college, but I recorded and posted my video.

Then I plugged it on the Twitter pages of my favorite autism charities. It even got the attention from some mainstream blogs, like *Mean Stinks*. I sent them my video and they responded with:

> Hi Jennifer! Thank you so much for sharing this video with us. We're so sorry that you experienced bullying and loneliness growing up, but we're VERY proud of you for staying strong, taking the higher road and always being yourself. You're quite an inspiration!!

This all goes to show that even if some opportunities are somehow lost, there will always be others, especially when it comes to projects you believe in and are willing to work for!

LESSON 30
Don't forget that it could always be worse

IT'S NOT EASY FOR MY MOM to be the mother of two autistic girls, especially when she sees families with typical girls who seem to have it easier. Autism has caused a lot of drama in my family, as when I had to change schools (twice) in the eighth grade or when Flora went to a chiropractor who was not very accommodating to her needs. It's even more frustrating considering Mom arranged a lot of biomedical treatments for us, from gluten-free diets to hyperbaric oxygen chambers, some of which did a lot for me but not so much for my sister Flora. For some autistic kids, biomedical treatment doesn't work at all, and working hard for nothing is never fun.

However, I'm there to remind Mom and Dad that things could be better, but also a lot worse. For example, a lot of parents of autistic children divorce—80 percent the last time I checked. Meanwhile, Mom and Dad have one of the best marriages of the twenty-first century. Also, my mom knows this one lady named Kim Stagliano who has no less than three autistic girls. While she loves them, raising them has been no picnic.

I'm not saying that autistic children ruin their parents' lives or anything. It's just that raising autistic kids is never easy. Kim Stagliano seems to be pretty happy for a woman who has to deal with three autistic girls and constantly gets trashed by guys on the Internet who don't like her autism blog. But that's another story.

In fact, my parents are close not "despite" having two autistic daughters, but partly because of it. And difficulties in life make good things that much more special.

LESSON 31
Good things come to those who wait

IN THE ELEVENTH GRADE, I was feeling very bored at home. The lack of schoolwork was starting to catch up to me. I didn't even have driver's ed to keep me occupied.

So Mom and Dad realized I needed a better school, but it took them a long time to find one. While they explored many options, I was growing more and more bored, wishing I had an exciting life. In fact, I wanted to be Taylor Swift.

I tried to cope with this problem constructively (sort of). I sent a letter to Tim Burton asking him to direct a movie based on the coolest cheesy eighties TV show, *Manimal*. I wanted to be in the movie as well, as the title superhero's stepdaughter. However, for some reason Tim Burton never got back to me. His loss!

In the meantime, Mom and Dad were in the process of finding a new school for me. It took a long time, but we finally found one that looked great. I especially liked the school store, where good kids got prizes every Friday. When the principal interviewed me he seemed a bit skeptical at first, but when I told him that I thought *The Amazing Spider-Man* was an allegory about autism, he decided to admit me.

All this goes to show that if you wait long enough, good things will come. And if you work at several things at once, some of them are bound to succeed.

PART VI
STRESS AND SETBACKS

LESSON 32
If you can't control it, let it go

BEFORE I ALMOST COMPLETELY LOST it in the eighth grade, I had difficulty juggling two activities on the same day. I was part of the Newspaper Club and the Student Council. My name had been put in a raffle for the Student Council, and that's how I got in. Having so much to do would have stressed out a neurotypical student, let alone an autistic student such as myself. I wanted to go to the Student Council meetings so badly, but Newspaper Club kept interfering with it.

At the first Newspaper Club meeting we discussed the superpowers we wanted. One girl said she wanted to make copies of herself. That would've been really convenient for anyone who has to deal with multiple activities!

When I missed Student Council meetings, I had meltdowns. One meltdown was so bad I had to leave school. I tried to organize a field day at school, but when it was canceled at the last moment because it was so wet, my heart broke. Over the year, I faced other similar disappointments, like not being able to go to a Diwali party because it was too rainy to drive.

Part of me thinks that if I had talked to the principal to get me out of Student Council, things might have been different, but at the time I was more seriously affected and couldn't really speak up. Over the years, I learned that some situations like these are out of my control. You just have to roll with the punches and not let the stress get to you.

LESSON 33
If it's too scary, don't do it

WHEN I ATTENDED A DAY CAMP, they had overnight trips to amusement parks for the older kids aged ten and up. When I was seven, I was incredibly envious of the girls who got to go on these trips. I couldn't wait to grow up!

However, when I was finally old enough to go on an overnight to Six Flags Great Adventure, I was a bit nervous, because I was scared of roller coasters. You know how some kids get upset because they're too short for rides? Well, for me, the exact opposite was true. Because I was almost five feet tall, the older girls felt obligated to invite me on all the roller coasters. My autism made it difficult for me to say no to some things, as I had difficulty expressing my true feelings. Therefore, I was kind of stuck riding roller coasters.

One of the rides was a log flume. It had a big drop, and I was pretty scared of it. I tried to offset my fear on the ride by thinking of exciting scenes from my stories, but I was terrified when the ride dropped. I screamed, "Mommy!" acting like someone half my age.

As a teenager, I enjoyed going to amusement parks with my friend Kurt. Now, Kurt is a total daredevil. He's even gone on Kingda Ka, the tallest, fastest roller coaster in North America! I've only been on a handful of the rides he has been on, but that's okay. I've learned that you shouldn't do things that make you feel uncomfortable, as I've had too many bad experiences with roller coasters. You have to trust your gut to make these decisions.

LESSON 34
Don't bite off more than you can chew

THE TRANSITION FROM HIGH SCHOOL to college was a difficult one, because there was a much heavier load of homework. I signed up for no fewer than five courses: Film, Theater, Writing, Italian Food, and Spanish. At first it didn't sound like too much for me, especially since they all sounded like cool courses.

As it turned out, just when I was being assigned a lot of reading, I found myself reading very slowly. I couldn't focus on the page. That's a common drawback of autism. I was treated for it, and my reading speed and comprehension gradually improved in college, but it took a while.

In the meantime, it was hard to juggle all five of my courses. The most difficult class was Film, because it had the heaviest reading load. I would even try reading as little as possible while still trying to grasp the gist of the passages. The homework and the stress kept piling up, to the point where the classes were no longer fun. I liked hearing lectures and reading about movies (*The Wizard of Oz*, for instance), but the stress kept me even from enjoying the film class. In Theater class, meanwhile, I forgot to read *Hamlet*. And I had a full email inbox, which was overwhelming.

Eventually Mom and I realized the workload was too much and that I needed to drop a course. I left the Film course, despite it being my favorite subject, because it was the most time-consuming. After that, college got much easier for me and I was able to keep up and cope with my course load. In the end, I had learned that there's only so much I can handle and that I shouldn't try to bend until I break.

LESSON 35
But take care of responsibilities and get things done

I SPENT MY FIRST YEAR of college living at home rather than a dorm room, which helped me adjust to the new setting, but there were still stresses I had to deal with there.

For example, one day I had some Spanish homework to do and I was babysitting my sister later that night. My Spanish professor gave me various assignments on various pages, which was confusing. They were fun, but puzzling. One of the assignments included looking up and listening to the Spanish song "Guantanamera." At first I thought I had to look up the original poem by José Martí, but I was wrong, and eventually found a version by the Fugees. (For those who don't know, the Fugees were a rap-reggae group from the 1990s—in other words, from back before rap music became stupid and plastic.)

I felt overwhelmed by the confusion the homework was causing, and on top of that I had to babysit my sister Flora because Mom was going to Back-to-School night at Flora's school. Normally, babysitting was easy, as my sister did nothing but play video games, but I had trouble coping because I was exhausted after finishing my homework. However, I hid it well until Mom gave us an early dinner. Then I started bickering with her. (Yeah, like normal teenage girls never do this.)

So after dinner, I decided to unwind. I called a friend to wish her a happy birthday. I visited a charity website. I tried to post a parody of a Facebook page on DeviantArt. (DeviantArt wouldn't let me.) I eventually decided to watch *American Dad* and call it a day.

Throughout college, I've had some really busy days. What I've learned from them is that I can't always adjust life; sometimes, I need to adjust myself to life instead and make sure to include the things that will help me deal with the stress.

LESSON 36
You can't run away from your problems

SOMETIMES, HOWEVER, STRESS gets to be too much, and the bad seems to outweigh the good. When this happens, you have to remember that running away solves nothing. I learned this lesson when I was ten.

I was a fairly levelheaded ten-year-old, but I was not without my fair share of issues. One night in June, I felt very busy, as I wanted to finish a school project before doing HBOT. Furthermore, I also had math homework, and math wasn't exactly my strong point.

I was doing my school project, but felt somewhat distracted, and it took a long time. Later, I tried to do my math homework. Since one of my sister's friends came over, I wanted to fit everything into one night, which was very frustrating for me. Dad had to review the material over and over again, which stressed out both of us. I was doing long division, which wasn't easy for an autistic ten-year-old who was more inclined to the language arts.

When I was finally finished, I told Dad I wanted to do HBOT. Unfortunately for me, he told me that it was too late that night. I felt furious because I didn't get everything that I wanted. I then tried to run away. Dad caught me, and Mom tried to comfort me.

"Please don't run away. Running away solves nothing," she told me.

"But life was easier when I was in second grade!" I cried.

"No, Jenny. You had difficulty in school, and you didn't have a lot of friends. Now look at you! You're doing well in school; you have friends; you have a lot going for you!"

The reason I got so upset was that I really wanted to do HBOT, because Mom was doing HBOT and she said it did wonders for her skin. I wanted to be pretty, as well as smart. Well, prettier, because Mom always reassured me and told me how pretty I was.

However, she was right about what I did. Running across the street would have accomplished nothing. I have to deal with my problems as they come.

LESSON 37
Stay on track and accept the setbacks

FOR MOST OF THE ELEVENTH GRADE, I was incredibly bored, because the school did not give a lot of homework. Basically, I spent the majority of time at home watching movies or surfing the web—I had a lot of energy that wasn't being directed at anything productive.

That's why I got super excited when I found out about the "Miss Teen New Jersey" contest. I talked to Mom and Dad about it, and they said, "Yes!" So I applied, and then I got a phone call from one of the pageant organizers. She asked why I wanted to do the contest, and I said, "Well, Mom told me about Miss Montana 2012 and how she beat autism, and I was inspired by her!" My mom had met Miss Montana, Alexis Wineman, at an autism conference, and I admired her. My parents pointed out that I could do the contest but it wouldn't make me famous. While I knew deep down that they were right, I didn't care. I wanted to be an autism icon, just like Miss Montana.

When I went to summer camp, I told some of my friends about the contest, in case they wanted to watch it on TV. Everything seemed to be going smoothly for me . . . until I came home and realized I forgot to fill out a form and had missed the application deadline for the pageant. I was so devastated that I cried all night. Not even watching *The Producers* (the hilarious 1967 version, not the lame 2005 remake) made me feel better. Getting your hopes up often backfires.

Still, there were still positive things that happened that year. I participated in another, more low-key beauty contest.

And I did not give up on my dream. Once I read an email where my mom wrote, "I hope we get the acting/modeling out of Jenny's head and get her to focus on her SATs!" *Yeah, good luck with that, Mom,* I thought. (Yes, I did snoop on my parents' email. Who doesn't?) But yes, I did eventually forget about beauty contents and refocus on my exams. You can't always predict the future; there will always be setbacks, so do your best to cope and move on.

PART VII
COPING

LESSON 38
Music can heal

T MAY SOUND STRANGE, BUT even when I was going through rough periods in my life, there was much I enjoyed. I loved listening to pop stars I admired and making "singer cards," which were basically trading cards with my favorite musicians on them. Music therapy can work wonders for autistic kids, be it hearing or making music.

As I've mentioned before, life in the eighth grade was tough. I attended three schools in one year, and even in the third one I was getting upset a lot and feeling hopeless. I also had no friends my own age.

Well, almost no friends.

My "best friends" were Avril Lavigne, Katy Perry, Gwen Stefani, Hilary Duff, and Britney Spears. I had an iPod stuffed with music, so whenever anyone asked, "What kind of music do you like?" I would say, "All kinds!" One teacher bragged that I liked oldies, and it wasn't that much of an exaggeration. I did like some songs from the eighties, like Madonna and Journey. (If you're a teenager today, eighties songs are "oldies.") I was always drawing pictures of my iPod, with my favorite musicians on the screen and the tagline "My iPod's got it all!" Hilary Duff represented pop music, Avril Lavigne represented rock music, Kanye West represented hip-hop music, and Britney Spears represented "dance" music. Sometimes, I would even draw Beyoncé, for R&B.

In March of that year, Mom and Dad enrolled me in an acting class. During the concert before the play, I got to sing my favorite song, Avril Lavigne's "I'm With You." It's a beautiful song about finding hope in a "damn cold night." I was able to sing my heart out, and it was then that my parents started to realize what a big impact music had on my life. Whenever Mom and I hear that song, we think about how much that song helped me get through my "damn cold night." It's a metaphor for feeling lost and alone—a metaphor for autism. I would love to sing it with Avril in concert!

And relating to pop songs wasn't limited to her, of course. Songs like "Stronger" by Britney Spears ("Now I'm stronger than yesterday, now it's nothing but my way") and "Change" by Taylor Swift ("The walls that they put up to hold us back will fall down") reminded me to keep my head up during hard times.

LESSON 39
Laugh and look for silver linings

Always look on the bright side of life.
  —*Life of Brian* (the singing and dancing crucifixion scene)

SPEAKING OF MISSED OPPORTUNITIES, in April 2014 (Autism Awareness Month, natch), the restaurant chain Chili's announced they were going to have a fund-raiser for the National Autism Association (NAA). Mom, Dad, my sister Flora, and I were all excited to have a dinner out for a great cause. However, our fun was ruined.

You see, the NAA was the victim of a smear campaign. Some people said they were anti-vaccine, which isn't true. Their fund-raiser wasn't about vaccines at all; it was meant to help autistic kids who wander away from their homes, like Avonte Oquendo, who a few months earlier had walked away from his school and drowned. NAA was supporting causes like Project Lifesaver, which gives autistic kids bracelets that send out a radio signal so the police can track them if they run away. My sister Flora wore such a bracelet, which our parents got for her after she disappeared and was found cycling down an interstate highway.

The reason that NAA was attacked was McCarthyism of sorts. Back in the 1950s, anyone who believed in social justice was called a "communist." Today, autism activists are often called "anti-vaccine," even when they're not. (I read *The Crucible* in theater class.)

At first I thought all the negative reaction would die down, but I was wrong. Eventually, due to outside pressure, Chili's caved in and canceled the fund-raiser.

When I found out I was extremely disappointed, and I called a "Hopeline" for teens with issues to talk about it. The lady on the other end also seemed upset about it. I also discussed it at school. I was happy to hear that people out there cared about the cause, despite all the controversy. Some of the comments that Chili's got on their Facebook announcement indicate that people were concerned about autism and they were angry at Chili's too. Fortunately, in reaction to the cancellation, more donations were made directly to the National Autism Association than they would have gotten from Chili's fund-raiser!

But the real fun came from fantasizing about revenge tactics for the people who made Chili's cancel. I imagined that we might make them wear "I love Justin Bieber" shirts or force them to watch awful movies, like *Twilight* or *Catwoman*. "Oh, Jenny, you're cruel!" joked Mom. While I know revenge solves nothing, fantasizing about it is perfectly fun.

LESSON **40**
If you don't get what you want, find productive ways to cope

ONCE, I WAS TALKING WITH MY PARENTS about one of my favorite television shows, *2 Broke Girls*. Unfortunately, the conversation strayed to what I thought was a rather unpleasant topic. You see, my parents do *un*glamorous autism activism, the kind that involves research and political action. It isn't pretty, and that bothered me. At first I cried that I wanted to be rich and famous, like Abigail Breslin. At this point Dad said, "I'm pretty sure Abigail Breslin wants to be Taylor Swift."

Then I whined that I wanted a Make-a-Wish Foundation for autistic kids with activist parents (like me), at which point Mom said, "Now, Jenny, the Make-a-Wish Foundation is for kids who are dying of terminal illnesses." So basically I was comparing autism to *dying of a terminal illness*. Kind of selfish, no? My mom told me that even though being a teenager was a drag, it didn't count as a terminal illness.

Ironically, the show *2 Broke Girls* is about a rich and famous socialite who loses all her money after her father is jailed for a Ponzi scheme, so she has to work as a waitress. In other words, once other people served her, now she has to serve other people. She was selfish until she became poor, and then she learned to help others.

So I decided to donate money to Make-A-Wish. I know I sound corny, but I felt good after doing good. All this goes to show that if you want something, instead of whining, be constructive about it. You may not get what you want, but if you help other people get what they want, at least you'll put your negative energy to good use. And hey, even if some of my dreams don't come true, at least these kids' dreams will.

LESSON 41
Make time for the things you like

WEEKENDS DURING COLLEGE can be strenuous. For example, one busy Sunday I was doing a report on a play I liked, *Top Girls*, about working women in the 1980s. I was also watching *Pretty Little Liars*, a show I enjoyed. I was in a rush, because I was getting a new TV and wanted to watch what I had taped on the DVR before it was too late. Oh, and it was the twenty-fifth anniversary of the fall of the Berlin Wall, which Mom wanted to celebrate because she was in Germany before it happened.

You see, on Saturdays, I usually like to watch old movies with my family. They run late at night, and then I like to listen to music while changing the posters in my room, as I'm usually too busy during the day to take care of that. Then when I wake up on Sunday, I like to read magazines to get ideas for what I'll be wearing that day, based on the style of my favorite musicians, especially Taylor Swift. While these activities are somewhat tiring, they also give me something fun to do over the weekend.

Most college students have experience doing homework over the weekends, but I wasn't really prepared for having so much of it. (You'll read more about that in the next lesson.) Mom bragged to all the people she knew about how I was doing so well in such a stressful situation. (Okay, so maybe I didn't always keep up with my homework at first, but that was because I was taking five classes, which was more than I could handle.)

While I often feel exhausted and overwhelmed, especially on Sundays, I enjoy keeping busy with my hobbies because they balance out the work.

LESSON 42
Life should have balance

WHEN YOU REALLY THINK ABOUT IT, having too much of anything, however wonderful, can't be any good. For example, during the tenth grade, when I realized how easy school was for me, I took advantage of having so much free time to surf the Internet and write *Backyard Sports* fan fiction. I couldn't really write fan fiction during previous years because I was too overwhelmed by school, and I also didn't know where to show it off.

By the tenth grade, however, I was attending an alternative high school founded by hippies during the 1970s. The teachers were very laid-back and often gave very simple homework assignments or none at all. This led me to think that I could stay up late online, because, hey, if I don't do anything in school, what's the point? I rarely had weekend projects, so I watched movies instead (Tim Burton was a favorite director). I also enjoyed listening to classic rock music (my favorites included old-school bands like Steve Miller, Elvis, and Queen) and reading about superheroes, like Zorro and Batman, whom I worked into my fan fiction.

Sounds good, right? No, I was getting bored. It didn't really hit me until close to the end of the tenth-grade school year, but I was trapped in this mix of pop culture, and it eventually got tiring. How often can you work on the same kind of fan fiction? You don't learn much. Sometimes autistic kids get fixated on trivia, and if we neglect more important academic topics, we can flunk out of school.

Finally, my parents sent me to a more challenging school for twelfth grade. It took a little while (okay, a really *long* while) to get used to it, but it was the right choice for me. It actually gave enough homework outside of school to keep me focused and helped prepare me for college.

So you see, real life needs to be a balance of work and play. Think of it as a couple of scales—you don't want either side to weigh more than the other. When you have too much of something you enjoy, you can't really enjoy it.

LESSON 43
Use your free time constructively

IN THE TWELFTH GRADE, I was so mentally exhausted from school and SAT prep that all I wanted to do after finishing my homework was to unwind online. Some of the stuff I did online wasn't so educational or constructive, however.

One time Mom and Dad found me on a website with reviews of *The Simpsons*. Mom was like, "Jenny, I can't believe you're looking at this!" Dad said, "Now, Jenny, when I was your age, I watched junk television, but I didn't read about it." I was pretty embarrassed about the whole thing, but found Dad's line to be very humorous. My parents weren't too happy with me reading about TV shows online, not even intelligently written shows that they also enjoyed.

Now, the main reason Mom was so upset about me looking at stuff like this was because I didn't do well on my SATs. Mom believed this was partly because I was feeding my brain junk.

Thing was, I enjoyed reading about movies and TV online, because I wanted to write cartoons when I got older, so I was curious about how other people might react to my cartoons. That's why I read negative reviews of cartoons like *The Simpsons* and *Family Guy* online. Of course, they were also really fun. I mean, positive reviews are fine, but the biting negative reviews are what's really entertaining.

However, I did read about some intellectual topics online, as well, such as interviews with Stephen Hawking. In one of them,

Hawking talked about throwing a party for time travelers. To test whether they exist, he sent the invitations after the party. He waited and waited, but no one came, so he came to the conclusion that time travel doesn't exist. That's Stevie for ya!

I also signed some petitions online to help autistic people and advocate for animals rights.

Eventually, Mom realized that not everything I watched online was junk. However, I learned that I should use my spare time in more constructive ways. I may not be working, but I can still do more intellectual things. After all, even if I do constructive things sometimes, if Mom and Dad only see junk, they're going to think I'm lazy.

LESSON 44
Be patient, because there are no quick fixes

IN THE ELEVENTH GRADE, I went through a phase where I liked to read a lot: *Percy Jackson*, *Hamlet*, Meg Cabot, and even the classic Winnie-the-Pooh series. Trouble was, I had minor OCD (Obsessive Compulsive Disorder) and always made sure that I read every book perfectly. That is, I made sure I read every single word, but I wasn't focused on the story. That was very strenuous for me, so I rarely read more than one chapter a day.

As I got older and my reading list grew, reading became harder. I was reading slower and slower, stumbling over each and every word. Basically, I had the reading skills of an eight-year-old. I would read "The dog jumps over the fence" as "The. Dog. Ju-mps. Ov-er. The. Fence."

I was mentally exhausted, but due to my SAT prep and more challenging homework, I couldn't stop reading. As the school year passed, I wondered if I really could handle it.

Eventually, Dad said, "Now, Jenny, we understand that this reading problem of yours is not entirely in your control. So we're taking you to see a doctor who can help." So in April 2014 Mom and Dad took me to an eye care specialist, who was finally able to correct my reading problem with some computer games that exercised my eyes. However, even that took a while. My final appointment was in January 2015, after my first semester in college had ended.

I learned that when you have problems in life, they can't be solved overnight. They usually take time to get fixed, and you have to be patient while you address them.

PART VIII

LIFE HAPPENS

LESSON 45
You can't replicate a one-in-a-million moment

History doesn't repeat itself, but it does rhyme.

—attributed to Mark Twain

IN THE NINTH GRADE, I started getting interested in the Beatles. I already liked John Lennon, because he reminded me of my favorite musician at the time, Kanye West. (Kanye had even more in common with John Lennon after he married Kim Kardashian several years later, as both men had similar taste in women.) I wanted to reserve some time every day to listen to the Beatles. Then I discovered that Mom had an old CD of kids singing songs, a few of which were Beatles songs. I was curious (and excited!) about the CD and wanted to listen to it.

When I played "Imagine," I realized how beautiful it was. I had listened to this CD as a six-year-old, but back then I didn't realize those kids were singing Beatles songs. Now it was like magic!

The next year, I wanted that same beautiful moment again. I used another CD from my distant past, one with *Veggie Tales* songs. Trouble was, it wasn't as special, because not enough time had passed for me to rediscover it. There was a five-year gap between getting the CD and when I "rediscovered" it, as opposed to the eight-year gap with the other one. Eight years is a bigger deal than five years when you're fifteen. I hadn't had as much time to "forget" it. And, of course, silly kids' cartoons can't really have the same

impact as the Beatles. So it was a good experience, but not *as* good
as finding the kids' CD with "Imagine."

I tried again with another CD in 2012, but since Hurricane
Sandy knocked out all the power, it didn't work. I felt like I was on
a treadmill of sorts, trying to repeat the same magic over and over
again just because something made me feel really, really good.

Then I realized that, as great as these moments are, they're
called "one-in-a-million" for a reason. You can't do them over again.

LESSON 46
Don't feel bad about the past

IN MIDDLE SCHOOL, I got upset a lot, obsessed over certain TV shows (like *Family Guy*), and took people's comments very literally. There was one boy in school named Henry who went on about how the books he read were better than the books I read. (Name changed to protect the snooty.) For example, when I was reading *Harry Potter* and he was reading *Maximum Ride*, he bragged that *Harry Potter* was only chosen for a children's literature award, while *Maximum Ride* was chosen for an adult literature award. Apparently adult literature is superior to children's literature for some reason.

One day in chorus class, which we took together, I started talking about *Harry Potter*. Henry told me I was being disruptive, which was true, but I thought he was joking, since autistic children often misread social cues. The teacher spoke to me about it after class, and I got upset. When I got home, my mom explained to me that there is a time and a place for talking about what I'm reading.

During my first year in college, I stumbled upon the letter my chorus teacher wrote to my mom. I felt kind of bad about it, but then I realized that it was a long time ago—six years, in fact! You have to leave all these negative things in the past, where they belong.

First, if you focus too much on the past, and not enough on the present, then you miss out on what's around you. Second, that was then, this is now, and you have an opportunity to make a great future, even if you can't change the past.

One strategy I use to stop focusing on the past is to try to focus on a positive thing closer to the present. For example, I might look up a news story my family was in and see what positive attention I got from that. I also like to remind myself that childhood was a long time ago and I was a different person then. For instance, I was very quiet and often prone to getting upset.

Today, I'm much more relaxed and social, and I have more friends. I'm involved in more student organizations, from anime club to the college newspaper. Like many teenage girls, I used to fight with my mom, but I don't do that (as much) anymore. Always remember, bad things may have happened in the past, but life gets better.

LESSON 47
Talk about your feelings, even when it's hard

OVER THE COURSE OF THE SIXTH GRADE, Mom often talked to me in the morning about controlling my feelings. I resented it a lot, as it reminded me of my issues at school. One morning, I got upset about it and she told me, "Sometimes we have to talk about things like this!"

I thought that she was being too hard on me. She decided to show she truly cared about me by offering rewards, like taking me to the movies, and eventually I calmed down.

Some years later, there was friction between me and a boy at school. One day I lost it with him and a few other students. It was so serious I stayed the rest of the day in "Room 6," which wasn't detention (well, not exactly) but rather a place where upset kids went to calm down. When Mom and Dad asked what happened at school, I refused to talk about it, regardless of how much they pressed me. I felt too uncomfortable to talk about it and worried that they would be upset at me. They still told me that I needed to work on my feelings, which is when I decided to make my list of 100 reasons to be happy: to show that I could still enjoy life even when I hated parts of it. You can see my excellent list in Lesson 27.

Eventually, I got much better at talking about my feelings. When I got upset about depressing things on the news, for example, I could discuss them. Sometimes I did so in rather odd ways, however. I would try to shut out the bad news by whining that I wanted to be a celebrity like Elle Fanning, Ariana Grande, or Chloë Grace Moretz.

I think I'm going to have to explain this one. You see, Mom refers to our autism activism as "underground" work, as it is not popular enough to receive mainstream attention, and that upsets me. Sometimes I felt like, because of what I had to put up with in my life, I was entitled to fame and fortune: in other words, the American Dream. The last thing I needed was being involved with something as gritty as the "underground." This view bothers my parents sometimes.

However, I learned that as long as I don't complain too much, talking with my parents about my feelings is perfectly fine and even beneficial. I also know how to be aware of the causes of my feelings—the real reason I'm upset is because I don't feel rewarded enough for my work, despite getting to meet Jenny McCarthy. You will read more about that in the next lesson.

When you talk about your feelings, you find a way to deal with them rather than bottling them up, and you feel more in control of your life.

LESSON 48
Keep your expectations in perspective

WHEN YOU'RE AN EIGHTEEN-YEAR-OLD SURROUNDED by successful people your age or younger, it can be easy to feel jealous. Two of my idols, Lorde and Malala Yousafzai, for example, are actually slightly younger than me, but both have already taken the world by storm.

Lorde is a pop star who's gotten really popular for having an unconventional style. She has her own makeup line, she was named *Time* magazine's Most Influential Teen, and she even got to write the soundtrack to the Hunger Games movie *Mockingjay*. Okay, so a lot of people didn't realize she was only eighteen, because her music and image make her seem twice that age, but even so.

I also sometimes feel envious of Malala: we're both young women involved with controversial causes, me with autism and her with girls' education, yet I'm unknown and she's beloved by the general public. However, Mom pointed out that it wasn't easy for her to get there. Malala was shot at the age of fifteen for going to school, and while everyone in America treats Malala like a saint, some people in her native Pakistan don't like her. By feeling jealous of her fame, I was ignoring the struggles she faced along the way.

While some teenagers (like myself) feel jealous of famous people, I have been trying to deal with my envy in a more productive way by deciding to do creative and good things that attract attention to myself. I'm already making a name for myself by writing stories and fan fiction and posting them on the website DeviantArt. I asked one of my DeviantArt friends to illustrate them, and he drew an image for me. He really went out of his way: in the description, he wrote a little section about me. He discussed my cultural preferences, from movies (*Despicable Me* and *The Hunger Games*) and television (*The Simpsons*) to music (Taylor Swift, Miley Cyrus, and Selena Gomez.) He also wrote about my dream of writing movie scripts. Basically, he was saying, "Look how awesome my friend is!"

When I showed his picture to Mom and Dad, they said, "That was a super card your DeviantArt friend drew. You already have a fan base!" This shows that even if you're not big and important, there will always be people who think you're important enough to be your fans.

LESSON 49
Everyone is no good at something

Everybody is a genius. But if you judge a fish by its ability to climb a tree, it will live its whole life believing that it is stupid.

—attributed to Albert Einstein

WHEN I WAS SEVEN, I got ballet lessons as a birthday present. At first, I thought it would be fun to dance around. After all, as Isabelle Wright from *Glee* said, "Every little girl starts out wanting to be a ballerina." (Okay, maybe not every girl, some are tomboyish. But that's none of my business.) Unfortunately, if there were any issues, however minor, I would get upset. For example, sometimes I would have regular ballet shoes when I needed tap shoes, and I would have a meltdown and refuse to participate.

But that's not even getting to the real issue, which was that I was just not interested in ballet. When you're an autistic preteen who likes to think outside the box and acts like a free spirit, you're not really into an extremely structured activity like ballet. I didn't talk much about ballet beyond "leaping across the room." In the sixth grade, the last thing I needed was to be put into a stuffy leotard and skirt once a week—even if my ballet instructor praised me. Mom and I decided that I should quit ballet that summer, especially after Mom saw my odd behavior at the big recital, like looking into a satchel that wasn't mine. In other words, I was too distracted to be involved.

I felt bad, as I wanted to be good at the things that "normal" girls did. But not being good at something doesn't mean you're worthless. In fact, there will always be something we're not good at or interested in, and we can't force ourselves to like it.

LESSON 50
It's not a perfect world, and sometimes you're late for John Oliver

BECAUSE WE HAVE PROBLEMS WITH EXECUTIVE ISSUES—doing what we're supposed to do when we're supposed to do it—autistic students can find college difficult to manage. My first semester had its fair share of long days. In my theater class, I had to read the play *The Three Sisters* by Anton Chekhov, do an oral report on its historical context, and memorize and perform a scene with two other students. Because I wasn't used to doing huge theater projects, I felt overwhelmed and drained. Mom reminded me that it was my first project, not my last, which made me feel better.

After classes, I had to attend a rehearsal, eat dinner on campus, and then meet my dad, who was going to take me to see John Oliver doing a stand-up comedy routine at a local theater. It was a very big day.

I often have a hard time finding my way around campus, so my dad and I didn't meet up in time to get to John Oliver. It was, as Alanis Morrisette says, like "a traffic jam when you're already late." We finally got there about halfway through the show. I don't remember much except some Jet Ski jokes.

You know how some people say, "You haven't lived until . . ." and then tell you about some wild unexpected thing that happened to them? That was my experience. In fact, it's the experience of most autistic teens. Because we find it hard to plan and juggle, everyday life seems more wild and unexpected to us than it does to other teenagers. I always felt like I was hanging on a thread. At the wrong moment, a sucker-punch would set me off. I could never just let go and relax.

But you have to deal with the unexpected. You can't always play it safe; you have to live a little. Sometimes you get stuck in traffic. Sometimes it rains on field day. You have to come to terms with it. It helps if you always save stuff on your computer, but lots of other things can go wrong.

For instance, Hurricane Sandy. We had to batten down the hatches, and then it hit . . . right before Halloween, no less. Because there was no electricity, we went over to my grandmother's, and I watched "The Rocky Horror Glee Show," which is how most sixteen-year-olds spend Halloween anyway. Even a disaster can have an upside if you have a plan B.

All these challenges have taught me a valuable life lesson: good things and bad things happen to everyone. It's not a perfect world, and sometimes you need to put up with rain before a rainbow.